loving person, a wholly delightful and vigorous boy.

DARK RICE is a joyful and poignant celebration of unloved children transplanted into love. It is a buoyant and unforgettable story for everyone — children, teenagers and adults.

About the Author

On Easter Sunday, March 30, 1975, Maria Eitz organized Orphans Airlift, an umbrella organization to get children out of South Vietnam before the North Vietnamese takeover. It was she who waited for the children-filled planes in San Francisco, including the plane which President and Mrs. Ford met. As executive director of Orphans Airlift, she, along with many volunteers, housed the children until they could reach their new homes.

She has long been familiar with the procedures of bringing orphans into this country: For the last four years she handled weekly arrivals from Rosemary Taylor's orphanages.

Since completing DARK RICE, she has adopted two more Vietnamese orphans, Moki and Aiyana. Aiyana was one of the infants airlifted to the U.S. on the same plane which President Ford met.

Maria Eitz is a graduate of Marquette University, Milwaukee, and now teaches theology and conducts retreats in the San Francisco area.

About the Illustrator

Fred L. Weinman brings an impressive background to this book. He has done commercial illustrations for many years — he has a fondness for architecture — and has illustrated four children's books. His line drawings in DARK RICE match well the loving touch of the author.

Front Cover: Illustrated by Fred L. Weinman.

Country Beautiful Corporation
24198 W. Bluemound Road
Waukesha, Wisconsin

ISBN 0-87294-074-8   Printed in U.S.A.

DARK
RICE

Dark Rice

by Maria Eitz

Illustrated by
Fred L. Weinman

COUNTRY BEAUTIFUL
Waukesha, Wisconsin

Country Beautiful Corporation is a wholly owned subsidiary of Flick-Reedy Corporation: **President:** Frank Flick; **Vice President and General Manager:** Michael P. Dineen; **Treasurer and Secretary:** August Caamano.

To Rosemary J. Taylor, with love

The Vietnam from which Jonathan came is no more. With the evacuation of children from Rosemary Taylor's nurseries in April 1975, the link we maintained between Jonathan's old world and new life is broken. But not all is lost to war; the children who arrived in America are a beautiful living gift that can be given to peace and to the future in our country and in this world.

This gift of life has been made countless times by Rosemary Taylor. I am grateful for having been a witness to her goodness and concern. I know that because of her effort and love for eight years in Vietnam, thousands of children will bring us closer to the brotherhood of man.

Thank you Rosemary.

List of Illustrations

War has too many children already and not enough arms to hold them, not enough milk to feed them and no lullabyes, just cries and whimpers of all those who are nobody's sons and daughters.

Prologue

Dear Sir:

We never met. We do not know each other. We are strangers you and I — and yet the thought of you has grown so familiar to me that not a day goes by when I am not compelled to think of you somehow. Though you do not know it you changed my life. The fact that unknown to ourselves, almost in spite of ourselves, we can affect change in the lives of others does not surprise me.

I always believed all of life is held together by a certain harmony, a certain order like water in a pond. And each human act, for better or for worse, is like the stone that thrown into the water moves the whole pond. Though the water will cease to move when the stone finds rest at the bottom of the pond, it may be that on its journey downwards it begets a new beginning.

Four years ago you fathered a child in Vietnam, sir, and he came to be my son. You planted life in the womb of war. It took root and grew and all the terrible efforts towards destruction could not stop hope from being born. You began a new life, and though you left it, it gathered strength enough to open its tiny mouth and cry.

In the beginning there was darkness for the child you fathered, sir. Nobody rejoiced over the birth of another boy child. War has too many children already and not enough arms to hold them, not enough milk to feed them and no lullabyes, just cries and whimpers of all those who are nobody's sons and daughters. Orphans are war's unhappy property yet war cannot deny their existence, their cries and whimpers. War cannot make them stop, not even with the most terrible noises. Some children persist with living. The child you fathered, sir, was among them.

For two and a half years he grew in torn places where death and need make things vibrate, and yet he clung to life with the stubborn endurance of a little tree. The will to live was greater in him than all the pain and want and need that held him. He bowed to necessities and took sand and drops of dew where there was no good earth and water, and he formed them into a stem and branches. Flowers he could not make. He did not even have the strength to fashion leaves big enough to reveal what kind of little tree grew there.

I took the little tree from Vietnam and planted him in the garden of my life. Sir, he is beautiful and covered with blooms now. I have never seen blooms quite like his. He is not an ordinary little tree. He is so strangely beautiful that I wish for the whole world to see him, but especially you, sir, for it is you who has the knowledge of the seed from which he came. What you gave and what is happening now in my garden belong to one promise that must live towards fulfillment. In a sense the promise you began is lost to you, and though it is given into my keeping, I do not own it.

Sir, to me the little blooming tree is a window opening on to new visions of future and hope and love. A future that did not come like a child would remain nameless and mean nothing to me. A child did come and his name is Jonathan.

One day soon, sir, when he needs to know about beginning, I will take him into the garden and fill his hands with good rich earth. I will tell him then: "You began like this, Jonathan, with goodness like earth." I will take a small seed and press it gently into his earth-filled hands, and I will say to him: "You see, it is because of a special seed in this earth's goodness that you can be you. The seed is important. If it would have come from a flower, a flower would grow. If it would have come from a tree, it would grow into one. If the seed would come from animal, that is what it would grow to be, but the seed came from love and so you grew, and one day you will be a man." I would like to say to Jonathan, "a man like your father," but that I cannot do.

Each child is heir to his parents' field of becoming and their toil and care of many years are the child's beginning. Only the son who knowingly takes what the people before him have prepared has the power to transform the field into a new harvest.

Jonathan is heir to the fruits of my life now — but I will keep alive in him the knowledge of a secret inheritance, your gift to him, sir. I will teach him to look beyond the fields and gardens I have walked in. It is important to me that Jonathan gathers knowledge about all growing things not only those which I have come to value. Can you imagine the loss if Jonathan would only recognize the flowers I have planted? What would he do with the trees and shrubs and bushes that may be his one day because of you?

But who are you, sir? You are the American soldier called to make war in a country far from your own. You are the hundred thousand men ordered to step out of your personal identities and into common uniforms, ordered to hand over arms and eyes and instincts to the machinery of destruction. You have a hundred thousand faces but only one name, American Soldier. And thousands of times you, American Soldier, tried to forget those indignities that follow when men are stripped of their individual humanities by stripping the impersonal uniform just long enough to feel the singular pleasures a man may feel when he empties himself, prompted not by command but by desire.

It is those moments when you tried to forget rank and serial number and remember your manhood, those very moments I cannot now forget because they are full of the begetting and bearing of countless children. You called up the future time after time and in thousands of little faces lies the answer to particular quests. You may not have believed in the possibility of an answer, Soldier, but it came all the same.

Now no one wants to listen. You withdrew. You left — but one cannot withdraw the question of creation because the answer is already given and lives in countless little children, in Jonathan too.

Each child wants to know one day if his coming was longed for. Each child deserves to be told. Because you did not tell Jonathan and all his brothers and sisters that someone waited for their coming, I must.

For as long as I remember I have loved
all the children who belong to no one
as my brothers and sisters.

I

The most longed for moments in my life never come with shouts of joy and bursts of color as I hope they will. They come quietly in their own time, in their own way, and sometimes it is only through tears that I suddenly see what I went looking for with laughter.

And so it happened that on an ordinary day in the summer of 1971 I was surprised to find a letter from Vietnam among my mail. There was a snapshot in the letter. I stared at it for a long time. It was a picture of an orphan child standing in front of a jeep, a small boy with pants much too big for him, bare feet and sad eyes.

It hurts to recognize the sadness in the eyes of a little child. I felt a deeply personal pain as I looked at the little boy from Vietnam. I remember a different country, a different war, but the same sadness burning in the eyes of children around me. I was an orphan once a long time ago in Germany, but there is no time long enough to make me forget the sadness I once knew.

As I grew up and away from the memory of my orphaned days, the desire to spare other children the experience of places filled with the cries of love's poverty grew with me. For as long as I

17

A small boy with pants much too big for him.

remember I have loved all the children who belong
to no one as my brothers and sisters. Whenever I
could I would take their hand and lead them to
warm places and kind people.

The day came when I was able to provide such
warm places, and I knew it was time to keep a
child's hand in mine, time that I, who am sister to
so many, become mother to a few.

All my life I worked for the moment when I would first say to a little boy: "You need not cry anymore. You are my son and I am your mother. I have come to bring you home." With my whole being I was sure that moment would come because I prepared for it all my life. I was deeply shocked to discover that what is a simple truth to me and a must born from the necessity of my life, seems to be a complicated problem to others and a question of forms and regulations.

The adoption agency declared my life an unusual case. They did not know which procedures to follow since my experience was so different compared to that of other prospective parents. And so I was told: "You must wait. Be patient with us. It is a question of forms and regulations, in time…maybe…you must wait.…"

Months went by and I waited. I waited everywhere, lifting my head listening to foot steps I could not yet hear, to the song that still slept in the singer, to the sounds of tomorrow. I waited and made ready for the little boy who needed me to be his mother.

The adoption agency did not give me reason to add to my hopes but it did not seek to diminish them either, and so they grew in their own way unhurried in the inexpressible depth of my longing. Some hopes are of an infinite loneliness and only a deep conviction can hold them and believe in their coming. I considered my feeling right even at those times when facts and arguments did not seem to be on the side of my hope. Unsupported and lonely my hope developed and led me slowly to new convictions.

19

I knew there was a child waiting somewhere at a place where children cry themselves to sleep each night. I heard them in my dream. And all day long I heard the hunger cries faintly like the waves in a seashell. I prayed that each day would bring me closer to the crying-place so that I could find my son and take him home and watch him go to sleep with a Teddy bear, not with hunger.

I wrote to orphanages around the world, and I went to buy a Teddy bear and a baby bed. My friends smiled at me. They never said what they thought. They just reminded me gently there was no need to hurry with those things. I did not hurry. I gathered the necessary materials slowly, one by one. Sometimes I wished I could speak of the things that lived deep within me, but there were so many questions I could not yet answer concerning them. I thought everything would become easier if I just simply prepared a room. Somehow I believed that if everything was ready for my son he would come. After all, everything in nature readies itself long before the arrival of new life. Is not the building of the nest the certain sign that there will be a nestling bird?

Preparing a place for my son was like carrying a secret and quietly moving towards the moment when it could be told. My students did not know about the cries of hunger I heard. But teaching was even more serious to me because I hoped I could teach them to listen to the deep and sad sounds in the heart of our world, so that there would be more who recognize the hunger cry no matter how far away. My friends did not know that the secret I carried grew heavier and heavier each day and sometimes I wanted to cry because I could not yet put it down into the little bed I had prepared.

And then the letter came from Vietnam. Father Joe, a military chaplain, answered my inquiry. What can I say about Father Joe? Think of night and you are afraid, and then you see a light. Suddenly darkness is a window with hope waiting behind it and you are not afraid anymore. Even if the light would go out you would not be afraid, you would recognize hope, even in darkness. That is how it is with Father Joe: He shines out hope and you just simply know there is a way.

Father Joe's letter told of the children's terrible need in the orphanages he had visited, of his wish to find homes for as many as he could, especially for the children fathered by GI's. They were born into a country where a different color, darker or lighter than the Vietnamese, marks the outcast. The children who are different from their mother's people are orphaned twice: They have no parents and no rightful place in their land of birth.

Father Joe's words made me see lines of hungry children holding empty rice bowls anxiously waiting for a spoonful of food. Would the ladle be empty again when it came to their bowl? And at the end of the line there are the children whose fathers have touched their skin with a hue of darkness. To be black in Vietnam means that you stand at the end of the line of hope. Father Joe assured me that if I truly wanted a child it would come to be since he knew of many children who truly needed a mother, like the little dark boy in the picture.

21

I knew there was a child waiting somewhere.

The boy in the picture! I looked at him again and again, astonished each time by the certain knowledge that I was looking at my son. There are no words fragile enough to describe the feeling, though it comes often now, the deep knowing. It grows deeper still and makes me believe both more and more simply in the importance of little things. They can become big and beyond measuring unexpectedly. That day I simply believed that living would be happier and larger for me and my little son. His bowl would not be empty. I would fill it with my life...I promised!

I wrote my promise down and sent it to Vietnam, confident that I would have to keep it. It is difficult, the promise to fill the bowl of a child's life not only with rice but with love, and I know with a terrible certitude that what is difficult will not be taken from me once I say "yes" to it seriously. I had never been more serious about any promise, and so I was sure that with my "yes" my son entered into the house of my living. Though I could not yet see him, I was sure of his coming long before it happened.

Father Joe did not seem to be surprised when I told him of my wish to make the little boy in the picture my own. He answered immediately and told me what he knew of my son. "They call him Hung in the orphanage. He is not yet two years old but already responsible for himself." Father thought there was something striking about the little fellow. "I suppose it is his eyes," he wrote, "they have drawing power." Little Hung stands at the end of the line in his orphanage because his skin is so dark. But he is fortunate—the boy next

23

to him never lets go of his hand. The other boy is a bit older, bright eyed and vivacious and never very far from the little one.

The sisters in the orphanage had told Father that it had been that way ever since Hung was brought to them as a baby only a few days old. It was the older boy who took care of the baby, who taught him all he knew and watched over him and wherever one went the other would follow. At night they shared the same sleeping mat. The sisters thought it might be so because the two of them were darker skinned than all the other children. The sisters complained that black babies were much trouble because no one wanted them and there was not enough food to go around.

Father explained that the first thing we had to do was to get Hung released from the orphanage. "We must offer food and money in exchange for him. Write the sisters and tell them you will give money to buy food for the other children if they let Hung go. Though the sisters do not want to keep these children, they will release them only for a price. Please send $50.00 and think of a name for your son.

"When the sisters let your boy go, I will take him to Saigon. I know a woman there. She will keep him until we can arrange to get him out of the country and to you. Rosemary will know what to do. If anyone can get children out of Vietnam at this time, she is the one. Rosemary will make it possible that one day you will see your son."

Little Hung stands at the end of the line in his orphanage because his skin is so dark.

I thought about a name for my son—a name is most important—it is a living word filled with history and meaning, and the gift of name is a serious gift since you call out certain hopes each time you call that name.

II

For the next few months the heartbeat of my life was measured by letters to and from Vietnam. The letter to the sisters begging them to let my son go was difficult to write because I had to struggle with the aching knowledge that they had named a price for the gift of son. I would have gladly given all I had because I cared. But to put a dollar value on care was something I found impossible to honor, and it was difficult to forgive the sisters who asked $50.00 in exchange for a son.

I did not put any of my ache into the letter. I told them of my hope instead, of the house and garden that are open like arms to receive the little boy. I told them how I lived and about my deep longing to share all I have with my little son. I sent them pictures and character references and I promised before God to love my son, to provide for him and protect him until he is ready to do these things one day for someone else.

I thought about a name for my son — a name is most important — it is a living word filled with history and meaning, and the gift of name is a serious gift since you call out certain hopes each time you call that name. To give a name to life is a sacred act for it is giving a name to mystery.

Yes, I thought about a name for my son. I looked for a name that is of goodness and strength, a name with growing room so that it can be filled by him who must live it. I looked for a name that one day would make known to my son the joy and gladness that came with him into my living, the gift he is to me, not to own, not to possess, but to give again one day when time sings the song of open doors and life calls to sons who are boys no more, but young men, able to inherit the care for our world.

I found the name for my son in a dream. It came to me like all knowing comes and in the middle of the night I wrote to Father Joe. "His name is Jonathan. It means, 'God gives a son'!" I did not tell Father Joe that giving this name to my son was like a covenant I made with God. But one day I will tell Jonathan, "Do you know that each time I call you, each time I speak to you and each time I name you in my thought, I speak of God's gift to me: That, my son, is you."

Father Joe liked the name. "It speaks of friendship," he said, "to become a friend like Jonathan was to David so long ago is still a wonderful challenge for anyone today. But for the moment our immediate challenge is to get your Jonathan away from here. Unfortunately you must go through an endless amount of red tape. You have to get the

President's permission for Jonathan to leave the country, but you also need the consent of the U.S. Immigration Department to grant him entry into the United States. Rosemary says this is best accomplished by writing letters to influential people you may know who will put their signature next to your request to adopt a child from Vietnam.

"Write to senators and congressmen and bishops. Ask for their statement of approval and then address yourself to President Thieu. You also need a number of character references from people who have known you for some time, a certificate of health, financial statement, and a letter attesting to your employment. The sooner you collect these materials the sooner we will be able to bring Jonathan home."

I wrote the letters and Father Joe sent pictures of Jonathan to keep me writing. Those pictures of my little barefoot son made it easy to address myself even to President Thieu.

I wrote to people who held impressive offices. Though it occurred to me that men charged with the running of cities and states and nations may not have the time to consider the case of one small boy and his empty rice bowl, I appealed to them anyway. Most of the men took time to respond on behalf of my small boy. I was glad because it is a sign of hope when men of importance are able to rejoice over one rice bowl that can be filled.

~ ~ ~

My longing for Jonathan was like a gate suddenly pushed open, and I who had only been a concerned onlooker of the war in Vietnam suddenly found myself deeply involved — and the bombs they talked about in the news report shook my life too.

I felt the terrible pull of the drama that is stretched taut between nation and nation: The energy and life spilled by the one who fathered my son and the burnt-out love of the other who carried him to birth. All I could do was believe in the hope and the love that is the child of peace and living still.

~ ~ ~

It became necessary to apply for citizenship papers in order for my little Vietnamese son to enter the land of his father. I, his mother, broke the bond I had all those years with the country of my youth. It was a difficult step for me because I had kept my German citizenship as the symbol of alliance with the pains and joys that had taught me all I know. To break bondage with the past is a small price to pay when it means the step into a certain future, and it was comforting to know there was no difficulty I had not been asked to pass through before my son.

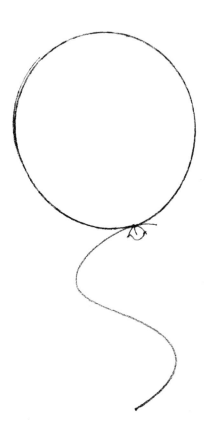

Because the girls wished me to understand
that richly brown skin invites the touch of pain,
I looked where I had found meaning clothed in
browns:...Leather is brown and nuts
and mountainsides and hands and bread.

III

The file with Jonathan's name grew fat with letters and copies of letters, and even in my dreams I climbed mountain after mountain of paper work. They seemed to grow in the path I had to walk to reach my little son. Each time I thought I was close enough to touch him, a new mountain pushed itself between us and I awoke shouting, "Don't cry, Jonathan. I will teach the mountains to grow small. I promise."

Paper work mountains grow smaller slowly, but teaching eased the waiting. One day when I came home from school, I found the letter that said, "Please buy a ticket for your son. He will come the end of July." I was so glad. I wanted to shout: "You see, Jonathan, the mountains are shrinking. A little while ago they were months high and now I can measure them in weeks."

Because my students had filled the many months of waiting with their warmth and presence, I celebrated with them the day I bought a ticket for Jonathan Eitz, a ticket for my son, a ticket to come home.

I will always be grateful to the girls who were my students in those days. Their interest and questions made it easier to project the coming of my son into each moment, and so each day was painful and beautiful like labor toward birth is meant to be.

"Why do you want a son who is black?" the girls asked.

"Because he is Jonathan."

They did not understand what I meant, but there was understanding in their smiles anyway. The girls tried to prepare me gently for those moments when society would frown at me and my son because we are not of the same color.

"There are many people who do not want to understand," they said.

"They will wonder about you, and you will hurt."

Until then the question of color had not been significant to me. My concern had been with what belonged to both of us. The likeness of circumstances shaping both his young life and my years had given me from the very beginning a deep sense of bondage with Jonathan. But my students were right. I had to acknowledge the external reality as well as the inner one.

My students, street-wise and given to realism, could not convince me, however, that the question of color is essential. After all, color does not determine sonship or motherhood. Why is it that people so easily lose sight of the essential meaning in favor of accidental details? Is it because the latter are more obvious? We call the obvious "fact" and we love to concern ourselves with "facts" rather than with meaning. Yet, does not meaning determine truth?

"Jonathan's skin is beautiful," Father Joe had written, "richly brown."

Because the girls wished me to understand that richly brown skin invites the touch of pain, I looked where I had found meaning clothed in browns: Earth is brown, sometimes deep and darkly so. Brown is the face of people who work the land. I have seen brown thoughts in the eyes of my friends, and brown and good to the touch is the hide of trees. Leather is brown and nuts and mountainsides and hands and bread.

I spoke to my students who ought to know best since they too were richly brown.

"What do you think about the color of my skin?"

One of them laughed with very black eyes and said, "I do not think of you as white. You are you and a good teacher."

"Do you think it is good for Jonathan and me to be mother and son?"

The girl looked at me a long time and finally answered, "I don't think so—I know so."

"Thank you," I whispered but wished there was something more I could have said. "Thank you."

"No need for thanks," she said, "it's true, but what was said about the hurt, that too is true."

~ ~ ~

It was supper time July 23 when the telephone rang. I went to answer.

"Long distance, Saigon," the operator said.

Holding the receiver I felt my heartbeat in my hand and in my ear too. It drummed so loud I could hardly hear, but I understood what Rosemary said to me, every word I understood with my whole being.

"Your son will arrive on Thursday, July 27, Flight 842, arriving San Francisco at 1700, your time. He is escorted by Captain Margaret Irons. She will wear a uniform and of course you will recognize your son."

"Yes," I said. "Yes, thank you; oh God, thank you."

I put down the receiver and my knees shook so much I had to sit down. Thursday! Jonathan is coming! I could measure the mountain in days! I ran into the kitchen. "Jonathan is coming on Thursday, this Thursday, Jonathan is coming home."

... to keep another life means to keep
the other's hunger and thirst in her own heart.

IV

Waiting for Thursday! I count hours irritated by the precision with which time marks all the faces of all the clocks. Something tremendous is about to happen. My whole being shakes in anticipation, yet I cannot move time. It will not skip even one minute for me. I feel bound. The drip-drip of time exhausts me. But feeling is not bound to the snail-pace-crawl of minutes. My longing can run and leap ahead to stare at any moment before it is named by the clocks. Ahead of me there is a new time clocks know nothing about—but do I? What do I know of mothering time?

I search my heart and walk once more through the rooms of my life to see if all is ready for my son. Suddenly I am afraid. I remember a time long ago:

I was a child then, just big enough to take care of a motherless lamb, or so I thought. The old man who had given the tiny creature into my arms had said,

"Will you keep the lamb? Will you give him all he needs? Even though I must tell you it is for the sake of the lamb you are a keeper and not for your own pleasure."

"Yes."

The child wanted to keep the lamb. She learned that it takes much patience and much loving. It was not enough to keep the little creature close when she longed for the comfort of closeness; it was not enough to feed him when she was hungry; it was not enough to give of her needs. The lamb needed more.

It happened that the old man came to the child in the night. He shook the sleep from her.

"Are you hungry, child?"

She felt drowsy with sleep. She heard the words, but what they meant this time, this hour, she did not know.

And the question reached for her again.

"Are you hungry, child?"

This time the words startled her. It was dark and cold and night, and words like those she heard did not seem to belong, not here, not now.

"Are you hungry, child?"

She sat up in bed. Without the warmth of sleep to cover her she felt cold and frightened. Then she felt the old man's hand on her shoulder. Surely, he would order the darkness and show her where to look.

"Your lamb is crying with hunger, child. I gave him into your keeping. Now I come to ask you to give him back to me so that I may feed him whom you do not love enough."

That night the child made her bed in the stable. After the lamb was no longer crying with hunger, he nestled close to the child who had brought comfort and comforted her who cried because she had not known that to keep another life means to keep the other's hunger and thirst in her own heart.

On Thursday someone will put a son into my arms, a son into my keeping. "O God, let there be room in my heart for all his hunger and all his thirst." Being able to address myself to God and to say "Father" now comforts me as once the hand of the old man had done.

...it is for the sake of the lamb you are a keeper and not for your own pleasure.

*And I sang for my little son and all the
children like him who learn to cry without sounds
because no one ever comes when they cry....*

V

Thursday! This is the day of my longing. I keep looking at the announcement I sent out to my friends:

Rejoice With Me
For This Is The Day
When God Gave A Son
A Promise Into My Keeping

His Name Is Jonathan
Born Dec. 10th 1969
And Given Into My Care July 27th 1972

Rejoice With Us!

This is the morning of the day. I calm my heart with effort, I watch the wind play with the branches of the tree outside my window. The wind makes me

43

glad. It will keep the balloon dancing. The balloon is for Jonathan. I will greet my son with a red balloon and a finger puppet lion who seems to smile.

I am a bit afraid of our meeting because an airport is such a strange place for birth.

They said the plane will be on time. I am early. The airport is crowded. I hold the balloon string tightly and look for an empty space among the strangers to fill with my waiting. The balloon pulls at me gently. I am not alone — joy is waiting with me.

A big plane carried my little son. A long line of people pushes itself slowly through the waiting crowd. There is a great noise all around me. I strain to hear my little son who comes from somewhere behind this noise, but all I hear is the beating of my own heart.

And then I see him. Jonathan! I never knew it was possible to feel what I feel this moment.

And then he is in my arms, my little boy. He leans against me quietly and weary. He is so easy to hold. It is wonderful to walk with the weight of son in my arms.

There are things Miss Irons tells me, but I do not listen very well. I bury my chin into soft curly hair and watch as my son takes the finger puppet off my thumb and puts it on his own finger. He wiggles it. Then he looks up at me and smiles.

"Hello, Jonathan." I kiss him and settle him more firmly in my arms. Then we leave the airport and I carry Jonathan home.

~ ~ ~

The hour of dusk when light gently mingles with light and shadows, the hour for poems and rhymes, was when we arrived home. I carried my son into his room and put him on the floor. He looked around, pointed to the balloon which had escaped to the ceiling, and smiled. The deep black eyes smiled too. He pointed to the truck and the blocks and the Teddy bear in the bed and smiled.

I watched him play for a little while and then I went to prepare a bath. My little son got up when I left the room and reached for my hand. He watched the water fall into the tub with interest. When I began to undress him, he helped without taking his eyes off the tumbling water. I lifted my naked little boy into the tub. He quivered and looked at me with fright. I coaxed him gently into a sitting position and watched him relax little by little, and when his hands discovered the sound they could make spanking the water, all his tiredness splashed away with clapping hands and laughter.

I looked at my son. His nakedness touched me deeply. He was delicate and beautiful even though his arms and legs were too skinny, his belly bloated from malnutrition, and scars marked his skin. My hands claimed the body of my son for caring as I washed him and dried him and dressed him for the first time.

He liked being held, but I had to shift his weight in my arms until he found the right position for hugging. And I remembered then that some children have to be taught about hugging and being

His nakedness touched me deeply.

held. It is like a foreign language to them, the language of care expressed by touch.

Jonathan found a comfortable place in my arms. And I held him for a long time before I put him into the crib. He looked at me long and still with enormous deep eyes, so black that I could not distinguish the pupils. I played with his hands and his hair and then I hummed:

> *Sleep well*
> *you are home*
> *my little son.*
> *You have come*
> *God's gift to me.*
> *O little son*
> *sleep peacefully.*

He closed his eyes and sighed and I slipped out of the room.

I leaned against the wall outside the door and I wanted to shout at someone, "Why did no one hug him? Why did he have to wait two and a half years to be hugged?"

But there was no one to answer me and no one I could accuse except the silence.

I waited a few minutes before going back into the room to look at my sleeping son. What I saw made me tremble. Jonathan was wet with tears. He quivered with crying but there was no sound, just tears cried silently and sobs without sound. I lifted my little one up to hold him tight, so tight. I rocked him in my arms and I sang to him all the thoughts that came:

47

Cry my little one
cry with sound.
I will hear you little one
Cry, my son, cry.
I will come little son
when you call with your tears.
I will hear you little one
always hear you little son.
Cry little one
Let me hear your tears my son.

And then he cried, small little whimperings and I cried too. He nestled against me and sighed and I watched sleep come and take the soft whimpering sounds and then the tears.

I rocked him and held him close to me all night. And I sang for my little son and all the children like him who learn to cry without sounds because no one ever comes when they cry, because no one ever answers them, they keep silent their call.

I kept watch all night. I listened to Jonathan's breathing and sometimes to the wind outside.

The wind, brother wind
he taps the window with a branch from our tree
and sings a song for you
and sings a song for me.

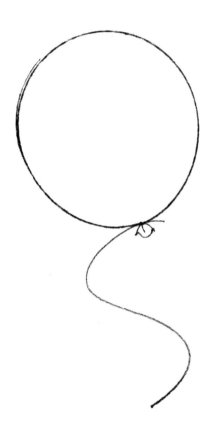

*... he looks at his food intently and I recognize
in his quick movements with the spoon
the knowledge of hunger.*

VI

Jonathan explores the house. After each run into a new room he returns to pat his crib. Jonathan's bed: Here he sleeps, here he lives. He smiles and smiles and runs out again, this time with the balloon in tow.

He brings the balloon to me with a flood of words I do not know. Among the sounds I soon distinguish "Kuna" and "Bom." I take the balloon and chase it with my hand.

"Balloon, come back balloon." And when I catch it by the tail I hand it to him. "Here is your balloon, Jonathan."

"Balloon," he says, trying the sound on his tongue. "Kuna, kuna, balloon."

I show him the photo album with all the pictures Father Joe had sent from the orphanage. My little boy is delighted when he recognizes himself in so many snapshots. "Jonnesan," he squeals, "Jonnesan." The album is a favorite thing for many hours till he finds his picture on the announcement.

"Jonnesan," he beams and puts four announcements in the middle of the floor and one on his bed for everyone to see.

"Jonnesan!" "Jonnesan!" "Jonnesan!" "Jonnesan!" Each card is touched and celebrated with smiles.

And then Jonathan wants to know my name. He points to my picture in the album and looks at me questioningly! "Kuna? Kuna?"

This is one of the moments I dreamed about when I would say to my child, "You are my son, and I am your mother." Why is it that now I want to cry?

Jonathan looks at me questioningly: "Kuna, kuna?"

"Mommy," I whisper and my heart leaps high.

Jonathan smiles and hugs my knees and runs off to play with a box and bag of marbles.

～ ～ ～

I watch my son eat. Perched high on his fire-engine-red chair he looks at his food intently and I recognize in his quick movements with the spoon the knowledge of hunger. Each little grain of rice is worthy of great attention.

Though Jonathan does not yet understand my words, I speak to him so that he may become accustomed to my voice and so that I may hear the promises I make because my gladness is so full it wishes to spill into other lives.

"Hunger was your teacher, my son. Hunger taught you to honor food — and you do, little one. I can see that. You need not go hungry anymore, my son, but I pray that neither you nor I shall forget our brothers and sisters who know hunger. Let us always be mindful, my son, of our brothers' empty rice bowls."

Jello: Jonathan never saw such food before. He smells and touches it and tries it with care — ah, he likes it. He beams at the wobbly bowl and spoons it up as fast as he can swallow. Don't worry Jonathan, there is more. See? I can fill your bowl again.

After he has eaten Jonathan climbs onto my lap for a wonderful moment of hugging. Jonathan spreads hugging joy. Oh my son, to be hugged by you is like springtime being quickened and smiled at by the rain. With the arms of my little boy I embrace the world!

～ ～ ～

I watch my son. All his favorite things appear in his bed. And very special objects are stored under the mattress. Jonathan shows me what he put there: a picture of mommy, a picture of Jonathan, two shiny pennies, and the finger puppet lion.

～ ～ ～

On his second day home I took Jonathan by car to the park. He sat in the back seat with a far away look in his eyes. Whenever I turned to look at him he smiled at me even though his eyes were filled with uncertainty and doubt.

We ran down the grassy slope to the sand box, the swings, and laughing children. But Jonathan did not laugh. He did not run to meet the children. He clung to my hand tightly and looked solemn with worry.

"No, no," he said, shaking his head at the sandbox, the swings, and the children. "No, no."

**And then with great shouts of joy...
he came running....**

We watched the children for awhile but Jonathan was not happy. He huddled against me and buried his face in my skirt. We turned and left the sandbox behind us. Jonathan relaxed with each step away from the noise of the playing children. And when there was nothing but a wonderful meadow before us he laughed and clapped his hands.

Jonathan wanted me to sit down. He patted the grass.

"Sit, sit!" And so I did. He beamed at me and then he turned and ran.

I watched my son run. He looked so small. I watched my son run away from me and my heart ached.

I did not call even though I wanted to. I did not run even though I wanted to. Something deep within me cried and pleaded, "Sit, sit." I watched my son run away from me knowing that my love must set him free. And though it hurt to stop the shout, I swallowed it and watched my son through tears.

He ran and ran a long way from me. And then he finally stopped and stood with his back turned my way. I watched and waited. Very slowly my little son turned. He was so far away I could not read his face. But I saw him lift his arms. He waved to me. And then with great shouts of joy, with squeals, he came running — and I ran to meet him.

I caught my son in my arms and swung him high. He shouted, "mommy, mommy," and pressed his arms around me so tightly I forgot to breathe.

This was our real meeting. My son came to me and called me to be his mother.

He symbolized ecstasy, such powerful joy that I ached as I watched his meeting with the waves.

VII

My house is transformed by the presence of
one small boy. Jonathan's eagerness to know
names of things has made me look at the familiar
objects in my life with new sight. It delights me to
learn from my son as I teach him words and names
of the things around us. Jonathan has a quick ear
for sounds. I discover that the easiest way to teach
him new words is by singing. Jonathan points
to something.

"Kuna, kuna, mommy?"

"I can see jello," I sing.

Then Jonathan tries it: "See jello."

When I sang about "yellow jello" Jonathan shook
with laughter and for hours he smiled delightedly
about such a happy combination of sound.

He refers to his room as "Jonnesan-your-room!"
His first lengthy conversation in English involved
this private kingdom, his room. We arranged yellow
daises from the garden for the living room. Jonathan
put each flower in the vase.

Jonathan put each flower in the vase.

"Dink water fower." Then looking at me he asked softly, "Fower Jonnesan-your-room pease?"

"Yes, my son, we will put some yellow daisies in your room too."

~ ~ ~

Jonathan greets all visitors with great enthusiasm and ceremony: "How you do, how you do?"

And then he takes them by the hand and leads them to his room. There he opens his arms wide in the middle of his room and shouts, "See, is Jonnesan-your-room!" He does not wait for any reply but comes dashing to my side, and thus protected he watches and listens and learns.

"Tell us about Jonathan," my friends want to know.

"What is he like?"

"What does he do?"

"Are there problems you encountered?"

"How did his past affect him?"

At these moments I wish my friends could have seen Jonathan when I took him to his first meeting with the ocean. The song of water made him dance with a joy so great that watching him made my body tingle. He symbolized ecstasy, such powerful joy that I ached as I watched his meeting with the waves. He looked so small against the sea, and yet from his small person there streamed such powerful joy that the great sound of water and his shout became like the clap of two hands. And passers-by stopped to watch:

"Look at that child," but all Jonathan heard was the voice born from water.

~ ~ ~

Sometimes he remembers things from the past. He trembles and hugs my knees tightly. Once on a walk through the woods a twig fell on Jonathan just as a plane had passed over head. He was terror struck. With wild panic in his eyes he slapped at his clothing. I caught him in my arms and held him tightly until he could see again that there were no flames, just trees swaying lightly in the wind. There was the rustle of leaves but no angry airplane. There were children laughing somewhere behind us but no screams and shouts of pain. Jonathan relaxed in my arms sighed with relief and hugged me.

～ ～ ～

Jonathan likes music.

"Lissen," he says. "Moosic."

My son picks up tunes and melodies like other children pick up toys. He hums to himself. He sings to me and to all his stuffed animals. He likes the sound wind makes. He laughs at the humming song of the refrigerator, the clicking sound that comes from the oven when it is heating, the bubbling perk from the coffeepot, the drip drip from the faucet. And then there are his own sounds, the rhythm he beats on the old milk can, on pots and pans and table tops. He sits for half an hour at a time touching the guitar in different places feeling the music vibrate, listening, smiling deeply.

"Jonnesan, Jonnesan, moosic man."

"I wonder which instrument you will choose one day to play your song for the world to hear, my son?"

"Moosic, zutiful moosic."

～ ～ ～

Jonathan approaches other children carefully almost as if he is ready to be pushed away by them, and when they make room for him in the sandbox, he is surprised and then jubilant with joy. When I hold another child for a minute or push someone else on the swing Jonathan grows worried. He pulls at my hand.

"Jonnesan-your-mommy. Go home, cour* Jonnesan. Jonnesan, mommy boy."

His lip quivers and his eyes grow huge and anxious. He watches me and does not like it when others come too close, not even Kippy, the dog. Jonathan considers Kippy a rival for my affection. He does not like it when the dog, jumping up and down with excitement each time we return from somewhere, licks my nose. To even the score Jonathan first hugs me, then he kisses me rather noisily, and after all that he licks my nose, too, turning his head triumphantly to make sure that Kippy has watched the whole ceremony.

"Kippy no belong mommy! Jonnesan belong is mommy boy."

With great fascination I watch Jonathan mope. Such a small boy, such a great moper. I am pleased about his moping ability. It shows strength of will and determination in a rather unhappy fashion. He sits in the middle of the kitchen floor, his eyes fastened to the ceiling, his back turned against me. Jonathan is on strike! Sitting down, pouting, he is terribly annoyed at me because I do not protest his

*Jonathan had picked up a few French words and he often used cour to express "for" and "with."

63

protest. I just simply let him sit out all his hurt feelings. Every so often I inquire if Jonathan is finished with his moping. He stares at the ceiling a bit harder and turns his back a fraction more against me. He sits for forty-five minutes fiddling with his shoes watching me out of the corner of his eyes. Little by little he inches his way closer to me and all of a sudden he bursts into smiles. After that we both forget the moping and talk about pleasant things like lunch or water or walk or flower or music.

Jonathan's favorite time is the hour before he goes to sleep. That hour we share only with each other in "Jonnesan-your-room." We sit on an island of togetherness filled with smiles and stories and hugs. We hear the voices and noises other people make like a soft ocean outside the door, background music for the things we do only with each other.

"Good night, my son. Catch a happy dream."

But Jonathan catches my hand instead: "No no go away mommy."

"No, Jonathan, I will stay right here in the house watching over you while you sleep."

"Good night, my son."

"Night night my mommy, tay here."

"Good night, Jonathan. God bless you."

"Night night my mommy, you too."

VIII

I am amazed at the speed with which Jonathan learns English. Words are his favorite toys — but much too soon they are no longer playthings, but tools he uses to help me see the world he came from. He picks out words carefully, almost as if they were material chosen by the tailor who selects colors and textures to fit certain personalities. Jonathan clothes old impressions and feelings that live in his roomy memory and offers them to my understanding. He tries to tell me of the things he used to know almost as if he understood that I need the knowledge of his yesterdays to prepare him better for our tomorrows.

"Vietnam hunger place. Hurt belong Vietnam. Little boy broken Vietnam. Gun can hurt. Vietnam hurt Jonnesan. No mommy Vietnam. Many, many children all broken, all cry."

For the first six months after Jonathan came home I awaken each dawn startled to find my sleeping son on the floor beside my bed. I gather him up

...I awaken each dawn startled to find my
sleeping son on the floor beside my bed.

gently and carry him back to the crib in his room. Sometimes he stirs in my arms and sighs, "Mommy belong Jonnesan."

I never hear him come. He never wakes me, and yet something does because each night before the birds begin to call the morning, I wake to find my son and his dream in my room. We do not talk about this habit of his until Jonathan no longer feels the need to get up quietly during the night and curl up on the carpet in front of my bed.

One day he said,

"Member when I was here early? I come to sleep in your room."

"Yes, I remember."

"Do you know why, my mommy?"

"Why Jonathan?"

"When you must go away and I am sleeping and you get out of your bed, Jonnesan is right here and then I always know."

"But you don't sleep anymore on my floor."

"I know." Jonathan smiles. "You never leave your boy when it is dark."

~ ~ ~

Washing his Teddy bear's clothes, Jonathan is busy at the bathroom sink, or so I think. He comes running.

"Look mommy, Jonnesan all better now. No more curl hair." He has wet his hair to make it lie flat. It is dripping. The drops seem strangely like tears.

"Jonnesan much better now. No good curl hair all gone. Mommy like Jonnesan much better?"

I put my cheek against his wet face.

"No."

69

Jonathan looks at me surprised. He does not believe me.

"Curl hair gone. Jonnesan all right now. No good curl hair all gone. See?" He wiggles his head in front of my eyes and places my hand on his smoothed-out hair.

"No good curl hair all gone, mommy. Jonnesan is good boy."

I hug Jonathan close to me, and his dripping head, and the pain he remembers because straight-haired children had scorned his curls. I hold my son. It is usually easy to comfort a little child. You make a circle with your arms around his life and you let only warm thoughts and comfort and laughter and smiles come in. And all the hurt that ever was cannot enter the magic circle that holds a small son. But Jonathan brings hurt even into my arms. He hurts because he believes the world does not like black skin and curls. He feels comforted in my arms but I wonder as I hold him how long I must hug him close to me before he feels safe enough to forgive the world who taught him to feel unwanted in his own skin.

I ask Jonathan to get the photo album with the pictures from Vietnam. We look at them together.

"Which boy do you like?" I ask him. Jonathan studies the children in the picture a long time.

"This one." He points to a Vietnamese boy.

"Has no curl hair. Is good." He looks at me and chews the edge of his lip.

"I like this one," I say, "and I want to be his mommy."

"Is Jonnesan. Has curl hair."

"I know. I think he is beautiful and I am glad he has curls. I like curls."

"Mommy like Jonnesan curl hair?"

"Yes, I do. Very much."

"Why?"

"Because curls belong to you. I like everything that belongs to you because I love you."

He looks at me anxiously.

"Black too?"

"Yes, Jonathan, black too. I wanted you to belong to me, not this little boy with straight hair or that one with white skin. I wanted Jonathan to come to be my son."

Jonathan hugs me tightly, so tightly, and then he laughs.

"Jonnesan like curl hair. Jonnesan like black. Jonnesan like belong to mommy. Jonnesan much good boy." His hair is alive with curls again and there are no more tearlike drops now.

～ ～ ～

"Little girl call Jonnesan chocolate, mommy." He studies my face carefully.

"Mommy like that name?"

"I like your name much better."

"Why girl call Jonnesan chocolate, mommy?"

"I think because both you and chocolate are brown."

"Brown is good, mommy?"

"Yes my son it is good to be brown."

～ ～ ～

A few days later Tammy, the little girl from across the street, comes to play.

He rocked himself back and forth looking out of the window though I am sure what he saw did not grow in our garden.

"Your little boy is black isn't he?" Tammy smiles at me. Jonathan shakes his head and pulls at Tammy's hand.

"No," he says. "I is a brown boy."

"Don't you think it is wonderful to be brown, Tammy?"

"He looks nice," she says. "I like to play with him best. He is my friend. But why is he brown?"

Jonathan answers for both of us: "Our Father made a brown boy because my mommy waited a long time for Jonnesan. He likes brown too."

～ ～ ～

We look at a book filled with pictures of children from all over the world. It is one of Jonathan's favorite books. He finds a picture he likes and then we wonder out loud about the children we see. But today Jonathan lingers over the first few pages. There is a pregnant woman standing in soft light surrounded by flowers. On the next page the woman smiles at her newly born baby. Jonathan is deeply interested. He moves back and forth between these pages for a long time studying each one carefully with his eyes and then with his hands.

"Baby was in woman's tummy and then he comes out?"

"Yes Jonathan. The baby was born."

"Did I grow in your tummy when I was very little?"

"No sweetheart. You grew in another woman's body until you were ready to be born."

"Did she smile when she saw me, mommy?"

"I don't know sweetheart, but I smiled when I first saw you."

73

Jonathan sat down to think about all this carefully. He rocked himself back and forth looking out of the window though I am sure what he saw did not grow in our garden. I watched my son and my heart ached. I tried to prepare an answer because I feared I knew the question yet to come.

"Where is the woman who grew me?"

"I don't know, sweetheart. Somewhere in Vietnam. She could not keep you, Jonathan. Do you know I am very glad that you grew because now I can be your mommy and you can be my son."

Jonathan looked at me deeply for a long time. He stopped rocking.

"I like you, my mommy," he said as softly as a smile.

That night I prayed for the woman who grew my son.

*It is usually easy to comfort a little child.
You make a circle with your arms around his
life and you let only warm thoughts and
comfort and laughter and smiles come in.*

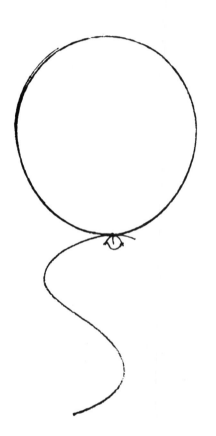

... our first summer was filled with so much
joy that it would take even more balloons than we
played with to let the world see the color and
songs that had come into my life with Jonathan.

IX

We knew each other one summer long. To me our first summer was filled with so much joy that it would take even more balloons than we played with to let the world see the color and songs that had come into my life with Jonathan.

But sometimes I wondered if one summer's happiness was strong enough to convince Jonathan that his Vietnamese experiences need not be repeated. In Vietnam Jonathan was moved frequently and sometimes changes had to be made suddenly without warning to him and the other children. The children were picked up and moved and strangers and strange places held them for a little while. Jonathan learned not to expect that things remain the same. He learned to pack things neatly so that everything could be moved in a hurry. He learned to be ready.

I saw this readiness many times in Jonathan's eyes, in his actions and his explanations.

"Come on shildren. Kick kick. Evybody go now. Find other house. House boken. Evybody go away. Koor (meaning poor) evybody. No more house. All big people go away. All gone."

As summer turned into fall and no one seemed to ready himself for a move, Jonathan grew restless. As he watched the leaves change color and drop from the trees and bushes, he grew more troubled. I heard him speak sadly to his favorite toy people.

"One day koor Jonnesan hab to go away."

My little son had quietly decided that it was he who had to move this time, for life without anyone moving he could not imagine.

"Do you want to go away Jonathan?"

"No, no mommy."

"Then why don't you stay, sweetheart. I don't want you to go away."

Jonathan hugs my knees and says, "Jonnesan hab to, mommy."

"But you belong to me, remember?"

"I know, but Jonnesan always hab to go."

"Why sweetheart?"

"I don't know. I don't know how works."

Jonathan's terrible sadness at those moments made my heart quiver. I would hug him tightly. "No one can take you away. You are my son and I am your mommy."

Jonathan crawled deeper into my arms and after much thought he said with a new hope, "Jonnesan hab to go away but I come back."

Jonathan's worries caused me deep concern, especially since they would now coincide with a short stay in the hospital which I could not postpone any longer. The doctors convinced me that the necessary surgery on his teeth and gums had to be done as soon as possible.

I prepared Jonathan carefully. I told him that we would get his teeth fixed pretty soon and both of us would stay in another house for just awhile.

"Jonnesan leeping in other house? In other bed?"

"Yes. But only for a very little while."

Three days before we had to go into the hospital I bought a big fire engine, much bigger than the one Jonathan had pointed out to me longingly. We put the fire engine in my closet and several times during the day we would go and admire it.

"When you go to get your teeth fixed the fire engine will belong to you."

Jonathan liked the idea. Everyone who came to the house was shown the fire engine in mommy's closet.

"Come see. Fire engine belong to Jonnesan soon."

When we were alone that night he turned to me questioningly. "Mommy, big hurt, big fire engine. Little hurt, little fire engine?"

I had not thought of it that way but I nodded.

"Jonnesan like big fire engine." But that was not the most important thing he wanted to know.

"Fire engine come with Jonnesan go away?" I realized that this very casual inquiry was of deep importance to my son and I thought long before I answered: "No. The fire engine will stay here and when Jonathan comes back with mommy, the fire engine will be waiting for Jonathan in his room."

He was delighted. He clapped his hands and made me tell the same thing over and over again.

The day before our hospital stay I took Jonathan to the children's ward so that he would not be quite so frightened the next day. Jonathan clung to my hand as we looked around. The nurse showed us the room we would stay in tomorrow. Jonathan took one look at the iron cribs and I felt his deep shock of recognition. There were two rows of little beds, some of them empty. Jonathan caught his breath sharply.

"Jonnesan tay here?"

"Yes, sweetheart. We will stay here tomorrow."

"Mommy tay here too?"

He was hopeful but not at all convinced. After all, the beds he had seen were much too small for a mommy.

We had to leave the house early Friday morning. But even before breakfast we moved the big red fire engine into Jonathan's room. He played with it, but not really. His thoughts were elsewhere.

"We go now? Mommy bring Jonnesan go away now?"

I packed his Charlie and Killy into the bag we were to take. Jonathan watched in silence.

"Koor evybody."

It was time to go.

"Bye-bye house."

Jonathan sat huddled on my lap in the car watching the rain drops roll down the windshield. I hugged my son, wishing he would cry tears of his own.

Admission went smoothly but when the lady put the name bracelet on Jonathan's wrist I felt him

We put the fire engine in my closet and several
times during the day we would go and admire it.

shake. He looked at me with pain and fright alive in his eyes. I had forgotten to tell him about the identification bracelet and we both knew he had a wrist band just like it when he came from Vietnam.

"See," I said. "It says Jonathan Eitz belongs to mommy, right here."

He studied the band with his far away look and sighed. Then Jonathan took my hand bravely and we walked along yellow corridors to the elevator that brought us to pediatrics.

The nurses fell in love with my boy.

"What a beautiful child." All smiled when they watched him and Jonathan smiled back. Jonathan moved cautiously, careful not to offend anyone. He responded with grave politeness to all the nurses' inquiries.

"No, thank you." Not for a single moment did he take his eyes off me.

"Jonnesan tay with mommy."

He did not like the crib the nurse showed him but he said to her, "Jonnesan tay here. I lub it." And then to me in a whisper, "Where mommy bed is?"

"I am going to sit right here in this chair. I can see you better."

It was time to prepare Jonathan for surgery. He did not even cry when the nurse gave the injections. He lay quietly on his stomach, his face turned towards me holding my hand tightly through the bars of the crib. As the injections began to take effect, Jonathan struggled with all his might to keep his eyes open, clinging more tightly to my fingers.

"My mommy please no go away."

82

As the injections began to take effect, Jonathan
struggled with all his might to keep his eyes
open, clinging more tightly to my fingers.

Finally his eyes fell shut. He looked so small, so very small, my son.

I helped the attendant wheel the bed into the elevator. Jonathan woke up when the elevator started to move. He looked at me with terror in his eyes:

"Jonnesan no like go Vietnam, please my mommy."

The elevator doors opened and someone pulled the bed out. I could not come.

"Jonathan, I am going to wait right here. Mommy is not going away, please sweetheart."

But Jonathan did not believe me. He turned his head away. I pleaded with the man in green not to roll the bed away just yet. I stood in the elevator and waited. Finally Jonathan turned to look at me and I saw his lips quiver.

The elevator door closed and I was trapped in a cage of loneliness. I closed my eyes but the darkness did not take away Jonathan's face and the fear in his eyes. I kept seeing them before me no matter where I looked.

"Two hours," the doctors had told me.

I walked around the hospital for two hours trying to forget and remember. After two hours the nurse told me that Jonathan was still in surgery and I would have to wait another hour or more. I no longer felt loneliness. I felt fear now. It was still raining outside. I watched the rain and though I understood burning thirst at that moment, the rain out there could not soothe the terrible fire I felt. I wished I could cry.

84

Four hours I waited and the nurse said to me, "He is still in surgery. I will let you know the moment he comes out."

I no longer burned inside. I felt much too empty. I could no longer see the rain. I could see my life like a desert, empty without Jonathan.

"O God, I will keep all my promises to you, but you cannot break the one you gave to me."

I waited two more hours. I do not wish to remember the pain of those hours, but before they were over I knew no matter what happened there would be a second child in my life. His name would be Nicholas, bringer of hope and joy.

～ ～ ～

I heard someone say, "Where is the mother of that little boy, Jonathan? She is needed in the recovery room."

I saw a terrified Jonathan caged in a plastic tent and wailing Vietnamese sounds as he whipped the mattress with his naked little body. Two nurses, bending over him very tall and green in their uniforms were trying to calm him. Jonathan shrieked. The sound cut into me deeply. Then he saw me. His small body quivered and grew still as the huge eyes gathered up my coming.

"My mommy, you come back," he whispered.

But before I could speak exhaustion had drawn him away.

He did not awake in the elevator on the way back to pediatrics. He did not wake up until several hours later and when he did he smiled at me.

I watched my son all night long and I loved him.

Thank you Our Father
for the gift of son
for the gift of being mother
thank you.
I will call a brother
and the promise carved from pain
shall be alive and bear a name
and be a son and be a brother.
Thank you Father
for the gift of son
for the gift of being mother.

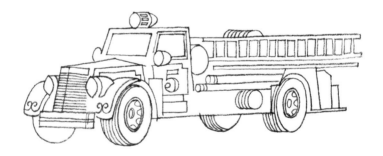

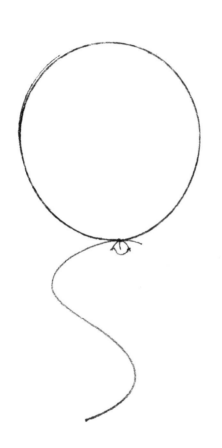

We walk hand in hand and I hear my heart sing with the early night wind. Jonathan sings for God but I listen too.

X

We are home again. Jonathan is happy, so wonderfully happy that everyone catches a bit of his radiance and turns it into smiles. My son walks about hugging things, the furniture, the dog, the daisy bush, whatever is huggable and within his reach.

"Jonnesan tay here. Jonnesan belong to mommy. No more go away never, never." His voice has deepened. It has grown richer with confidence like flowers grow richer with sun.

For weeks Jonathan is so bouncy with gladness that it is difficult to hold all of him. He is like a balloon in love with the wind, like a butterfly married to dance. It is a time to celebrate belonging for Jonathan. And for me it is a time to gather strength while I gather laughter and wonderful moments.

There are our walks in the late evening. We look for stars and the moon and jump over shadows. We touch dark leaves and wet blades of grass. We watch the lights go on and we try to look behind the dark curtain of moving clouds. We walk hand in hand and I hear my heart sing with the early night wind. Jonathan sings for God but I listen too.

My son walks around hugging things....

Our Father, Our Father
one day when he was happy
very much
he made the sun
and threw him up
high in the sky
very much high
and there was some left
and he throws up all the stars
many, many stars.
Our Father likes stars
and I do too.

On weekday mornings Jonathan's happiness is clouded when he sees me get ready for school. He has never liked my leaving for school. He has never said anything about it. Looking at me sadly he just puts his shoes on the wrong feet and asks, "This is wrong way?"

"Yes Jonnehan."

Knowing that I will not leave until he is fully dressed, he will sigh and slowly switch his shoes. But now he says, "I wish you tay in my house. I wish you be teacher with Jonnesan right here."

"But I need to go, sweetheart. I promised my students I would come today."

"I know," he sighs, "but my heart is sad about that."

"Please, Jonnehan, help me keep my promises and kiss me good-bye so that I can go to school."

"All right. But do big shildren know you is Jonnesan's mommy?"

I am sure my students know because this gift of son is a secret so great I must share it with everyone.

～ ～ ～

Jonathan talks and talks and I love the things he says:

"Here mommy, I will share you with my tea."

"Is alright. When your hand is tired you can use my other hand."

Once he discovered his reflection in the metal lid of a container.

"Look," he says. "Do you want to see into yourself?"

"What will I see, Jonnehan?"

"You see who you is, mommy. You see self who mommy is."

～ ～ ～

It is Advent, the warm time of evenings by candle light and soft Advent songs. My little son sits on my lap. He has candles in his eyes and he is wonder in my arms. This is the time when hope lights candles and teaches a small boy new songs. This is the Advent of a life and my hope burns strong.

Each morning we open a new window in our Advent calendar and Jonathan counts the days to his birthday. He will be three on December 10th and "much more bigger."

"I is growing upper and upper. No more red shoes. Now I have brown shoes. Member when I use to disn't? I is your much more bigger boy now. Are you glad about that? One day when I much bigger, after three, you know what I will do? I will show my heart to you when he is this big and zutiful."

Jonathan has grown indeed. He stands almost a head taller now and I think it is time to take him out of the crib and buy him a big bed of his own. To make the switch easier I promise Jonathan that I will sleep with him the night of his birthday in the new big bed. I buy the bottom part of a bunk bed and Jonathan watches excitedly as we paint it blue and white.

The night before his birthday Jonathan can hardly wait to go to sleep. I put him into the big bed and he looks so small. An hour later when I go back to check he is still awake.

"You are supposed to sleep Jonathan."

"I know," he says brightly. "I thinking how is when mommy is sleeping right here next to your boy." He pats the place where I am to lie.

It is very late when I am finally ready for bed. Jonathan is asleep but smiling still. I try to slip under the covers without waking him and I try to keep my night thoughts very quiet. But then I feel a hot little face against my arm and a wide awake voice in the darkness.

"I like you, my mommy. I like to touch your skin that belongs to you. May I please listen to your heart go up and down?"

What can I do? For the next few hours I am showered with wet kisses and exclamations of joy.

"Jonathan, it is time to close your eyes and go to sleep."

"I will, mommy. I just looking at you."

"But it is dark in here."

"I know, mommy. I looking with dark."

"Please, sweetheart, go to sleep."

"I will. I close the eye."

"Good night, Jonathan."

"Good night, mommy-sleep-with me." And three breaths later, "I like feel mommy's face. Are you leeping? I like leeping with you. I like mommy warm in my bed." That night there is very little sleep for the two of us.

In the morning Jonathan finds candles in his toast and presents under the kitchen table. He claps his hands and smiles and sings, "Happy birthday to Jonnesan" all morning. And in the afternoon we go to see "The Nutcracker Suite" ballet at the Opera House. Jonathan watches the performance transfixed. When the toy soldiers battle the mice he shrinks into his chair and searches for my hands.

"Guns, mommy. They have guns."

And when one of the mice falls Jonathan shouts, "Oh dear, one mouse is broken!" Throughout the rest of the performance he wants to know, "What happened to the mouse that was broken? Where did he go?" It is a good thing that the dance of the dragon makes him forget the fate of the broken mouse — at least for several hours.

Before going to bed that night he whispers, "I will tell you a secret, mommy." I bend close to him so as to catch it all.

"You my friend, mommy."

"I am?"

"Yes, you am very much." And to make sure I surely know it Jonathan kisses me. It is not a secret kiss but a loud and triumphant one.

~ ~ ~

Before Christmas we have a special little guest. Rosemary Taylor has asked if I can keep a Vietnamese baby girl until her new mother can come to San Francisco to take her home.

"Baby tay here? In Jonnesan house?"

"Yes, sweetheart, until her mommy can come and take her home."

"I see," Jonathan says. Biting his lip he studies my face.

I go to the airport and wait for the same plane that had brought Jonathan. I wait for another mother's child with the knowledge of Jonathan in my heart.

A young GI carries her off the plane.

"She is pretty sick," he says. "But once she tried to smile."

Leah is such a tiny little girl, ten pounds and one year old. She has developed a bad rattling cough. She is covered with cold sweat and her tiny hands try to hang onto air. Leah's eyes are huge. And though she can not sit by herself she can study faces and the world with deep knowing. "Your little sister, my son," I think. "She is hungry for love like you."

We arrive home. I put Leah down on the living room floor. Jonathan looks at her and the baby looks at him. It is as if they recognize each other. The tiny girl bursts into a smile. Her hungry face

95

gleams and with her whole body she reaches for Jonathan. Jonathan holds her hand and kisses it. Then he bends over her and gently like a father he kisses her forehead and touches her face.

"Baby come from Vietnam. Is all right baby come from Vietnam. Soon a mommy will take you home."

I have to leave the room because the presence of Jonathan's knowledge mingled with the knowing of this tiny little girl burst my heart.

We feed Leah, and bathe her, and dress her. Jonathan watches with care. Leah's head is always turned so that she can see Jonathan. It is good this way. My little son blesses her new beginning.

A few days after Leah has come and gone again Jonathan says to me, "One day mommy and Jonnesan pick up little shild has no mommy. Put shild come-from-Vietnam in little bed and tay here. Jonnesan and mommy take care of little shild. And then he has mommy and Jonnesan."

I pick up my son so as to see the thoughts behind his eyes, and say, "Can you share your room, Jonnehan?"

"I can," he answers without hesitation.

"Can you share your toys, Jonnehan?"

"I can," he says. "But little shild maybe no like fire engine. Is pretty big fire engine."

"Can you share mommy, Jonnehan?"

"I can," he says, leaning heavily against me putting his arms around my neck. "But my mommy belong to Jonnesan ever and ever."

I write to Rosemary in Saigon. I tell her that Jonathan is sleeping in a big bed now and that we both would love to put a little brother into the empty crib. Can she please help us find a boy who is looking for a mother and a brother?

I send the letter and when I tell Jonathan he hugs me and says, "I know, mommy, Jonnesan already know."

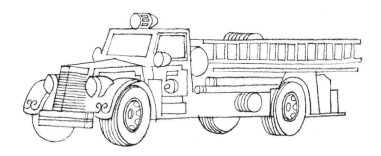

Waiting for Nicholas is indeed like waiting for Christmas except now there are daffodils and cherry blossoms and blooming trees and spring winds to fly kites high up high.

XI

My heart sings high when I am glad
my heart sings low when I am sad
my heart sings middle size when I am happy.

Jonathan sings. All things seem easier because of his songs. Even the paper work, the step-by-step procedures to find a brother for us, seems less difficult because Jonathan turns everything into songs.

"Hello mailman. Did you bring my brother today? Do you have Vietnam letter in your big pocket? I see you tomorrow, Mr. Mailman."

We sing and walk and play in the park. We go bumbling among Eucalyptus trees blowing soap bubbles. Jonathan calls them "bumbles" and he loves to chase after them. When we sit on the log near the meadow to catch our breath we sometimes talk about out little brother.

"I think we will call him Nicholas. Do you like that name?"

"Is almost like Christmas. I like Christmas very much, mommy."

Waiting for Nicholas is indeed like waiting for Christmas except now there are daffodils and cherry blossoms and blooming trees and spring winds to fly kites high up high.

Jonathan loves the spring and all the songs of newborn life. The children's zoo has a new crop of baby animals. Jonathan counts the many brothers of the little pig. The goat has four children now but the chicken has too many brothers to count.

Jonathan tries to hug them all. But then he crawls into my arms and whispers, "Jonathan like to be by self, mommy. Is all right, mommy, if he does not have a brother."

The spring days are growing longer and Jonathan works on the hole that he has made in the backyard. It is a wonderful hole, a special kind. Jonathan fills it with his imagination and it becomes peopled with wonder. I once loved a hill in Germany and I understand my son's love for a very special hole in our backyard. Becky and Clair, Jonathan's playmates, understand the magic hole that he has made. The three of them play beside it for hours. It pleases Jonathan when the little girls fill the hole with flowers. But each time Clair and Becky have to go home, Jonathan is sad because he likes their help with his games. The thought that a brother stays even when Becky and Clair must go is comforting.

When the girls have gone Jonathan gazes into the garden and ponders over lunch. "Maybe a brother can help with my hole."

The fire-engine-red high chair stands empty now. Jonathan sits on a booster chair at the table. He likes being big. He tells everyone he will share "his zutiful red chair with somebody's other boy one day, but not yet."

Being called to brotherhood is a strange and mysterious happening. There are comforts as well as troublesome sides to it.

"Only one boy suppose to belong to mommy. You cannot hold two boys very well, mommy."

I show Jonathan my two hands, one to put on his head, one on Nicholas'.

"I have two hands, sweetheart. I can hold two little boys very well. You will see."

Jonathan remains doubtful and cuddles closer.

"You can hold both Charlie and Dandelion, can't you?"

He runs to get his two specially loved animals.

"I know what else I can do, mommy. I can be a teacher same as you," he smiles. "I can teach my brother." This idea delights him and to try out how it feels he lines up all his toy people "to esplain how all works." Then he wants to know, "when it is tomorrow, will my brother come?"

"No, Jonnehan, not tomorrow."

But one morning there is a letter from Vietnam in the mailman's pouch. And now we look at the picture of our brother. My heart trembles and for a long time I look into the eyes of the sad faced, half naked, barefoot little boy. Twenty months before I felt like this holding the picture of my son, trying to shrink time and space so that it could be time to hold this son in my arms and carry him home.

"Jonathan, come and see. This is Nicholas."

Jonathan looks at the picture and sighs. "He is Vietnam boy, mommy. He has no shoes, has nothing. He is scared I think, mommy."

"What do you think we should do, Jonnehan?"

"I don't know, mommy. He can have my other shoes."

"I know what we can do, Jonnehan. Let's celebrate and make this a very special day."

That night I take him out to eat in style. Red-jacketed waiters seat us at a table for two with flowers and candlelight.

"Who are the red men?" he whispers.

"They are waiters," I whisper back.

"Oh," he says, and then after a moment's thought —"I don't know what they are waiting for."

As I gaze across the table at this son of mine, he appears so beautiful that I wish I could paint him forever and ever onto the walls of my heart. I see faintly behind him the long-ago face of the frightened little child crying without sound, and clearly now I see the face of Nicholas, somber with fear.

"You is thinking bout my brother," Jonathan says softly.

"Yes, sweetheart."

"I is thinking bout my brother, too. Are you glad mommy?"

"Yes, Jonnehan, I am glad."

"I am glad bout that too," he says climbing on my lap for a bit of heart-to-heart silence filled with the waiting for Nicholas.

~ ~ ~

Jonathan writes a letter.... He addresses the
envelope... to Our Father. We tie the letter
to the balloon string.

On July 27th we celebrate the anniversary of Jonathan's arrival. We buy a red balloon. Jonathan writes a letter about a little boy and a balloon. He addresses the envelope with big scribbles to Our Father. We tie the letter to the balloon string. We drive high up into the mountains, Jonathan and I and the balloon. We watch the balloon carry the letter into the sky beyond the fog.

"Oh," Jonathan says holding my hand tightly. "Oh, mommy, will Our Father smile? I hope he can catch the letter."

On our way home Jonathan sings,

> *Our Father we like you*
> *we sing*
> *we bring balloons*
> *me and my mommy.*
>
> *Our Father I like you*
> *you teach birds*
> *you take good care of people*
> *one two, one two little boys.*
>
> *One day we take you to a special place*
> *and we sing for you*
> *mommy, Jonathan, and Nicholas too.*

*...I wished very much I could take
Jonathan with me for my own comfort
since feeling my little son's hand in mine
is the most assuring warmth I can think of.*

XII

Almost a year later, May the 9th, was an ordinary school day for me. Glad about the sunshine and blue skies, I kissed Jonathan good-bye and drove to school. My students were cheerfully absent-minded and mindful only of the day count until summer vacation. But since we liked one another, they settled down for some work eventually. During block seven in the middle of somebody's insight, a voice from nowhere interrupted. "Miss Eitz, are you there?" I was, but in my bewilderment did not know to whom to declare my presence. The class did it for me.

"Yes, she's here. What do you want?"

"Emergency. Telephone. Please come to the office."

The voice fell from the ceiling and set my heart racing. O God! Something happened to my boy! I ran down the long hallways to the office. I dialed the number the receptionist handed to me. It took me some time before I understood that I had called the Pan Am office.

107

After I managed to properly identify myself, the person on the other end said, "Ah, yes, your son is arriving on Pan Am Flight 842. Saigon asked us to notify you."

I was stunned and stood there for a time, not knowing what to say or think. One of the ladies in the office offered me a glass of cold water and urged me to sit down. She tried to assure me and said kindly, "I hope the news is not too bad."

It was their turn to look bewildered when I burst into laughter and almost shouted, "Gosh, no. It's wonderful! I'm about to be a mother again."

I returned to my class and just when I started to explain to them what had happened, the voice in the ceiling said, "Fire drill B, fire drill B, evacuate school."

A bomb scare. All I could think was, "It is a boy, not a bomb. It is a boy. Nicholas is coming home."

I left the school without waiting to find out if the bomb scare turned up a real bomb or if the whole thing was just a prank. But Nicholas' coming was real. I had to go home to Jonathan. The long wait for a brother had turned into a sudden arrival, and I wondered if such suddeness would not be too difficult for my son.

I picked Jonathan up from his nap. I kissed his nose and told him something very wonderful was going to happen and I needed his help to get ready for it.

"Maybe we can have a tea party?" Jonathan said. He liked tea parties. We would sit on the floor with a tray of tea and cookies between us and tell each other happy things.

"That is a good idea," I said. "Let's have a tea party and then we can decide what color balloon I shall take to the airport because today Nicholas is coming home."

"Oh," Jonathan said, his head bowed low because he suddenly had difficulties with the buckle of his shoe. I managed the buckle for him.

"Thank you, my mommy. I member when there was a red balloon at the airport and a little lion too."

Jonathan chose a yellow balloon for himself and a red one for Nicholas. I decided not to take Jonathan to the airport because I did not want to pain him. I thought it would be better to bring Nicholas home where Jonathan felt sure and unthreatened. It would also be better for Nicholas to be held and hugged by me alone for just a little while. Though I knew I had made the right decision, I wished very much I could take Jonathan with me for my own comfort since feeling my little son's hand in mine is the most assuring warmth I can think of. Though I was joy-filled to go toward the meeting with my second son, close by, like a brother, I felt fear. What if Nicholas did not want me? What if Nicholas.... I never permitted myself to finish the thought. But even an unfinished thought can weigh heavily.

I hugged Jonathan and kissed him good-bye, and then the balloon and I left for the airport. I was an hour early and so I drank endless cups of coffee in the airport coffee shop watching the balloon bob in the slight breeze. The balloon was noticed by other children and they smiled. One little girl came to the table and asked in Spanish if she could not have the balloon.

"The balloon does not belong to me. The balloon is waiting for a little boy."

She did not like the answer, and she watched, disappointed, as I left the coffee shop with the balloon still bobbing along beside me.

Because there were four other children that came with Nicholas and his escorts from Saigon, the children stayed on the plane until all other passengers had deplaned. I went onto the plane to find my son. He stood in the aisle curiously trying to see where all the people had disappeared to. He saw the balloon and burst into the most beautiful smile I thought I had ever seen. The escort looked at me warmly and said,

"Good luck with your new son. Do you know I would have loved to keep him? He has such a wonderful personality."

I carried Nicholas off the plane. He was delighted with the balloon. For the next half hour he was content pulling the string, laughing and smiling, the envy of the other children. There he was, my Nicholas, chasing the balloon, tripping over his feet, not being used to shoes. I caught him in my arms and a wonderful feeling burst in my heart. "Oh, Jonathan, I think some sunshine has come to stay with us."

～ ～ ～

I carried Nicholas into Jonathan's room and put him, balloon and all, in the middle of the floor.

I carried Nicholas into Jonathan's room and
put him, balloon and all, in the middle
of the floor.

Jonathan tries to catch an escaping wave and
he can not understand that such a big wave
fills his pail not quite half full.

Jonathan had been sitting on his bed, hugging apprehension and Charlie.

"Hello, sweetheart," I said. "I brought you your brother."

Nicholas smiled at Jonathan and pointed to the yellow balloon which had escaped to the ceiling and was dangling its string like a tail alive with feeling. Jonathan tried to catch the yellow balloon and when he did he brought it to his brother. I tied a piece of LEGO (small building blocks) on each balloon string to keep them from floating out of reach, and before long the sun-filled room bounced with the shrieks and laughter of two little boys who had become fishermen of balloons.

～ ～ ～

And now it is summer, the barefoot season, the time most happily spent at the beach conversing with wind and waves and two little boys. I lie on a couch of sand and watch the boys at the edge of the sea. They dance in and out of the field of my vision with plastic pails and hands filled with treasures left behind by the water. Jonathan tries to catch an escaping wave and he can not understand that such a big wave fills his pail not quite half full. He carries the water carefully and pours it into the ditch his brother has built. Then they both lie on their stomachs to better see the goings-on in their own private little ocean.

The sand and the sun warm me and I look dreamily into the present, but no matter how wonderful the warmth of a summer day can be, the warmth that I feel comes from somewhere deep within, and it spreads from where I lie through my

114

arms and over the sand to the edge of the sea, to the castles and ditches two little boys have built.

The water dances with light. I half close my eyes to better see what happens in front of me. It is an amazing thing, so much more beautiful than any dream. I see two little boys holding hands and hugging laughter because the tunnel they made carefully digging into the wet sand, one from each end, did not collapse.

␣ ␣ ␣

Not so long ago these two little boys did not know one another and now they are brothers. Jonathan stands a head taller than Nicholas. He can see farther and he can help his little brother.

Jonathan sees a piece of driftwood. He runs to get it.

"Don't worry, Nicholas," he says, "I is your brother. I totect you."

"Here Nicholas. I found a much better shovel."

Nicholas beams. He finds words difficult but Jonathan understands his smiles.

"You are welcome."

Not so long ago Nicholas did not know the meaning of "brother" and "mother" and "happiness," and the words he did know were alien to the world that the two little boys are building before my eyes with sand and drift wood and water and seagull feathers.

Not so long ago Nicholas did not know what to do with a spoon. He did not know what to do with toys. He would bang the floor, the chair, the bed, and would tear at his clothing and shout. Little by little he edged his way into play, following his brother step-by-step, and now he is home safe and no longer a stranger in the land that little boys inhabit with their imaginations.

Jonathan is happy that it is so. He likes to play king and it never worked very well without someone his size who could be queen. He likes to play teacher and now he does not have to look all over the place for a student. He likes to play fire chief but someone ought to run the fire engine just in case a sudden fire happens somewhere.

There are occasional moments when Jonathan resents the burden of brotherhood. Once Nicholas wore Jonathan's old tiger pajamas and everyone laughed because of his brother's antics. Jonathan did not laugh.

"I don't like tigers. They hurt my heart."

"Oh dear," I said. "I am very sorry to hear that."

"Yes," Jonathan says. "And you know what else? They hurt my feelings too."

But most of the time brotherhood is a marvelous thing. The two boys complement and enhance each other.

And now they survey what they have built in the sand. Jonathan kneels and looks at the mound before him, sideways. Nicholas squats in Oriental fashion across from him, pondering his side of the mountain of sand.

"I know," he squeals. He pats the mound carefully before decorating it with a string of seaweed.

"Good idea." Jonathan likes it.

He looks around for more decorator items. There are none close at hand. Jonathan runs off. But

116

before he returns with more seaweed, he stops to dance with the waves for a little while, climbs the big boulder to stare at the seagulls, draws some doodles in the sand with a stick he found, and then using the stick like a conductor, he directs the waves and the wind and the seagulls to fall together in harmony. He practices a sandpiper walk for a bit and sits down to see on which toe the seashell he found will fit.

Meanwhile, Nicholas pats the mountain. To compensate for the lack of seaweed, he tries a row of holes by pressing his finger into the sand. Occasionally he looks up to see if his brother is coming back yet. He does not try to follow Jonathan. He does not venture far from my side. It is as if someone had drawn an invisible line in a circle around us. Nicholas stays within the margin of safety.

Content to pat the sand and delighted about the way sand feels, he fills the waiting with chatter. I look at the brothers with sun in my eyes and the wonderful knowledge that I am their mother. It seems to me like a miraculous wonder that the three of us belong to one another.

Jonathan is coming back with seaweed draped around his shoulder and trailing from his hands. Nicholas greets him with shouts of laughter, and I wish I could turn into a seagull and fly high into the sky and fill it with circles of joy because I am so very, very happy.

117

He climbs the big boulder to stare
at the seagulls....

Epilogue

Sir, that his coming was longed for I will be able to tell my son with my life and all my love. But there is so much I can not tell him. I tremble at times at the thought of the questions Jonathan will bring to me concerning you. You were the bringer of a great gift but you left without explaining the meaning of your gift. Since what you gave sprang from the depth of your person, no one but you will know its meaning.

I tremble at times because you are not there to comfort my son, to help him when it is time to leave the comfort of my arms. I tremble because Jonathan will be more alone than other sons in the face of the world.

Is not a son all the father was and that which the father did not become? Is not a son future as well as return of the past? I am the mother of his future but you are the father of his past. Jonathan must live his life feeling both our voices speak within his heart.

I know that there are the twin voices of parents in all sons, and all sons reflect in their song father and mother. But other sons come to know whom they reflect because they know the real images of both father and mother.

Jonathan does not know you, sir. He must search for you in the faces of all black men. I tremble at times at the thought that he might meet you and you will not know it. Sir, are you mindful of small boys who look at you with their heart in their eyes?

Please, sir, be kind to them. Speak to them of strength and courage so that my son, who must discover who he is, will also discover who his brothers are because of you. You fathered a dreamer, sir, for a child who watches always is called a dreamer. Speak gently to wide-eyed boys. Do not shatter their visions with differences but gently lead them to that which makes whole.

God bless you,

Jonathan's mother